101 Cooles
Do in /

CW00833331

Introduction

So you're going to Australia huh? You lucky lucky thing! You are sure in for a treat because Australia is truly one of the most magical countries on this planet.

This guide will take you on a journey from the major cities like Sydney, Melbourne, and Perth, right through to some of the more isolated parts of coastline and beautiful national parks that you'll find dotted around Australia.

In this guide, we'll be giving you the low down on:
- the very best things to shove in your pie hole, from incredible street markets through to fancy restaurants in Sydney
- incredible festivals, whether you would like to listen to the smooth sounds of jazz in Melbourne or you'd like to dance all night in the Australian bush
- the coolest historical and cultural sights that you simply cannot afford to miss from places in the desert with Aboriginal rock art to museums that tell the story of immigration in Australia

- the most incredible outdoor adventures, whether you'd like to get close to nature on an outdoor safari or you fancy raising your heartbeat with a white water rafting adventure
- the places where you can party like a local and make new friends
- and tonnes more coolness besides!

Let's not waste any more time – here are the 101 coolest things not to miss in Australia!

1. Go Surfing on Bondi Beach

When you think of the quintessential Australian, your mind might well wander to somebody with shaggy blonde hair, carrying a surf board. And to be honest, that's not far off from the truth. If you want to try your hand at being a real Australian, it's a great idea to head over to Bondi Beach in Sydney to hit those waves. You'll find plenty of surf schools on that particular stretch of coastline so that you'll soon be riding the Bondi waves just as the locals do.

2. Dance, Dance, Dance at Stereosonic

If you are serious about dance music, then you need to know about the Stereosonic festival in Australia. And there is absolutely no excuse not to attend, because this festival has instalments in Sydney, Melbourne, Perth, Brisbane, and Adelaide. The line-up for the festival improves every single year, and last year there was DJ and dance music talent from the likes of Major Lazer, Clean Bandit, Armin van Buuren, Diplo, and loads more exciting artists besides.

(http://stereosonic.com.au)

3. Spend the Night Camping at Taronga Zoo

Taronga Zoo is the city zoo of Sydney and it's a fantastic day trip for the whole family, where you get to say hello to animals from all over the world. But if you would like to take your zoo experience to the next level, you should think about staying at the zoos luxury glamping accommodation, Roar & Snoar. The experience includes a night time safari, an all you can eat buffet, and sleeping with the animals in nature. *(Bradleys Head Rd, Mosman NSW; https://taronga.org.au)*

4. Enjoy the Tropical Paradise of Orpheus Island

If your idea of a perfect getaway is to enjoy island paradise with clear waters and fine white sand, you need to know about Orpheus Island. The vast majority of this island is a protected national park, and there is just one resort there, the Orpheus Island Resort. It has 42 bedrooms, and that means it's pricey and exclusive, but if you want to treat yourself, it will be a trip to remember forever. Imagine having the 30 beaches of the island practically to yourself.

5. Explore Australia's Migration History at the Immigration Museum

As a cultural city, Melbourne is a place with no shortage of fascinating museums, and the Immigration Museum might just be the most fascinating of them all. This museum helps to put real faces and real stories to Australia's history of immigration over the last 200 years. You'll learn why newcomers to Melbourne left their homes, how they arrived in the country, and the mark they have made on Melbourne and Australia.
(400 Flinders St, Melbourne VIC;
https://museumvictoria.com.au/immigrationmuseum)

6. Have a Cultural Break at the Adelaide Fringe Festival

If you love nothing more than to be entertained by different kinds of shows, you should know about the Adelaide Fringe Festival. Unbelievably, this is the second largest annual arts festival in the whole world, and that makes it a must visit festival for culture vultures. Across the course of 24 days and nights in February and March, locals and visitors are treated to over 900 shows, mostly of new writing. This is the place to really feel Australia's creativity, and check out some cutting edge work.

(www.adelaidefringe.com.au)

7. Have a Fishing Adventure on the Murray River

Yes it's true that Australia is a country full of exciting adventures, but sometimes the most pleasant thing that you can do is sit by the edge of the river with your fishing rod in the water while waiting for a catch. If that sounds like heaven to you, you need to become acquainted with the Murray River in Australia. There are many species of fish in the river, but the big prize has to be the Murray cod, which is actually the largest freshwater fish to be found in the country.

8. View the Whole City From Sydney Tower

Sydney is a beautiful city, but you can't fully appreciate how awesome the city is from the ground. To get an incredible panorama of the whole city, we can recommend ascending to the city's highest viewpoint in the Sydney Tower. Once inside the Sydney Eye, you will have a 360 degree vantage point of the whole city, and you'll be able to take in the harbour and the mountains in the distance. You can also be treated to a 4D cinema experience up there to experience Sydney in a way that you've never experienced a city before.
(100 Market St, Sydney NSW; www.sydneytowereye.com.au)

9. Stay on a Pottery Producing Farmstay

If you fancy avoiding overpriced hotels on your trip to Australia, and you'd like to have a more interesting and authentic experience when it comes to accommodation, an alternative option could be the Barkala Farmstay in New South Wales. On your stay there, you will be welcome to wander the 8000 acres of land with its pigs, cows, and horses, and there is even a potter's studio where you can try your hand at spinning the potter's wheel and making a clay masterpiece.

(Dandry Rd, Coonabarabran NSW;

www.barkalafarmstay.com.au)

10. Discover the Aboriginal Rock Carvings at Kakadu

For us, Kakadu National Park has to be one of the most special places in Australia. This is because it is probably the best place to see traditional Aboriginal rock art in nature in the whole world. This art dates back to around 20,000 years ago and provides a fascinating glimpse into Australia's Aboriginal population from thousands of years gone by.

(https://parksaustralia.gov.au/kakadu)

11. Take in a Show at the Sydney Opera House

The Sydney Opera House might just be the most iconic building in Australia, and perhaps even one of the most recognised structures in the world. It's impressive enough to see the Opera House on the landscape of

Sydney Harbour, and it's even better to get up close, go inside, and watch a show inside the building. Over 1500 performances are hosted inside the building annually so you have no excuses. Whether you would like to attend a poetry reading, a symphony performance, or watch a ballet, there will be something for you.

(Bennelong Point, Sydney NSW; www.sydneyoperahouse.com)

12. Say Hi to Koalas at Cohunu Koala Park

Koalas are, of course, an animal strongly associated with Australia, and we're pretty sure that you'll leave Australia with a sad face if you don't get to have at least one koala interaction during your time in the country. And that means that you need to find your way to Cohunu Koala Park, which is located close to Perth. Visitors can have their photos taken holding a Koala, which has to be the selfie you have always dreamed of.

(Lot 103 LoNettleton Road, Byford WA;

http://cohunu.com.au)

13. Treat Yourself at the Margaret River Gourmet Escape

Australia doesn't have an incredible reputation as a country of culinary delights, but you might be persuaded to think otherwise if you visit the Margaret River Gourmet Escape, one of Australia's culinary events of the year. The festival takes place in November each year and attracts chef talent from around the world. At the festival you can take part in cooking classes, you can sample organic food from the region, sip on Australian wines, and all while taking in the incredible scenery of the river region.

(www.gourmetescape.com.au)

14. Find Some Peace in the Chinese Friendship Garden

Sydney is a great city because although it has all the trimmings of a 21st century cosmopolitan urban hub, it also has plenty of spaces where you can chill out and relax, and the Chinese Friendship Garden has to be one of the best of these spaces. The gardens are symbolic of the good relations between China and Australia, and inside you can find tall bamboo plants, glistening waterfalls, and there is even a tea pavilion where you can enjoy a traditional tea ceremony.

(Pier St, Sydney NSW)

15. Have an Artsy Day at the Museum of Contemporary Art Australia

When you think of the countries in the world most famous for their arts cultures, Australia might not be the very first country that springs to mind, but this is not to say that there is no visual arts culture to be found there, and this is very apparent as soon as you walk through the doors of the Museum of Contemporary Art Australia in Sydney. The museum has collected over 4000 works from Australian artists since 1989, and the collection comprises drawings, paintings, sculpture, and moving images.

(140 George St, The Rocks NSW; www.mca.com.au)

16. Rock Out to Indie Beats at Ding Dong Lounge

Melbourne is a city that really comes to life at night, and if you fancy spending a night on the town with some cool live music, Ding Dong Lounge is the venue for you. If you want something fancy, it mightn't be somewhere you'll love, but if you want a true rock n roll feel, you'll fall in love with the place. On any night of the week, you can discover homegrown music talent, whether in the form of a punk band, an electronic DJ, or a heavy metal outfit.

(18 Market Ln, Melbourne VIC; www.dingdonglounge.com.au)

17. Take a Day Trip to Cockatoo Island

One of the unique things about Sydney is that it is a harbour city that plays hosts to islands off the coast. One of our favourites of these islands is Cockatoo Island, and it's the ideal place for a day trip outside of the city centre. While the island used to be a place for people who had committed crimes on the mainland to be punished, it's now an altogether less grizzly place, and if you feel like having the full Cockatoo Island experience, there are camping and glamping opportunities.

18. Fill Your Stomach at Queen Victoria Market, Melbourne

If you want to get to grips with any city, you have to understand its market culture, and without a doubt the most iconic market in Melbourne is the Queen Victoria Market. This is the only surviving 19th century market in all of Melbourne, and these days it's mostly a place where people buy fresh produce and chow down on street eats. For a breakfast of strong coffee and handmade pastries, there's nowhere more pleasant in the city.

(513 Elizabeth St, Melbourne VIC; www.qvm.com.au)

19. Visit the Stunning Bungle Bungle Range

Australia is a country full of unique landscapes, and the Bungle Bungle Range has to be one of the most unique we have ever seen. Located in the Purnululu National Park, these beehive shaped towers are made from sandstone and conglomerates, and they date back to around 370 million years ago. From a distance, you can see clearly defined orange and black stripes covering the rocks, and as you get closer, you'll find a hidden world of gorges and pools by the Bungle Bungles.

20. Have a Hiking Adventure on Mount Wellington

Australia is a country full of epic landscapes and plenty of hiking and climbing opportunities, and one of the most popular spots for a breathy hike has to be Mount Wellington. Even though this can be a challenging hike, it doesn't have to be, because there are well marked roads and even buses that can take you halfway to the top. Just be sure to bring your winter woollens because there is normally snow at the top of the mountain. If you're lucky, you'll ascend to the peak above cloud level and see the fluffy clouds beneath you.

21. Take in the Artworks at National Gallery of Victoria

Melbourne is, at its heart, a cultural city, and so it should come as no surprise that you can find lots of awesome galleries there. Perhaps the most important of them all is the National Gallery of Victoria. This must visit gallery for art buffs has an incredible collection of Australian artworks, including aboriginal art and artefacts, colonial art, impressionist art, and also modern and contemporary works.

(180 St Kilda Rd, Melbourne VIC; www.ngv.vic.gov.au)

22. Spot Dolphins Off the Coast of Jervis Bay

As an island nation, Australia has a huge amount of coastline, and that means a lot of marine life. If you'd like to explore some of that marine life for yourself, Jervis Bay is a great place to settle down for a few days. Located on the coast of New South Wales, this bay is said to have the whitest sand in the world. And as if this wasn't a good enough reason to pack your bags and visit, it also has a huge population of bottle nose dolphins. There are many tour companies that can take you out on the water so you can see them up close.

23. Explore the Wineries of the Yarra Valley

For wine buffs, Australia is one of the greatest countries in the world for a vacation. If you want to explore Australia's wine country on your holiday, a trip to the Yarra Valley is non-negotiable. The cool climate of the area makes it the ideal place for growing grapes for Chardonnay, Pinot Noir, and some delicious sparkling wines as well. One winery that we particularly love is the TarraWarra Estate. You can enjoy tastings there, there is a beautiful outdoor restaurant, and, of course, you can purchase some bottles of wine to take home.

(11 Healesville-Yarra Glen Rd, Yarra Glen VIC; www.tarrawarra.com.au)

24. Peruse the Aisles of Old Bus Depot Markets, Canberra

Although Canberra is a capital city, it doesn't quite have the cosmopolitan vibe of Melbourne or Sydney, but it's still well worth a visit if for the Old Bus Depot Markets alone. This indoor market is the kind of place where you can find anything and everything, and we think it's an awesome spot for some souvenir shopping. Open every Sunday, you'll find clothes and accessories, china, jewellery, and there is even a gourmet food hall so you won't have to worry about going hungry.

(21 Wentworth Ave, Kingston ACT; http://obdm.com.au)

25. Say Hi to the Little Penguins of Phillip Island

Honestly, which animals are cuter than penguins? Err, Little Penguins! And there is a huge colony of these insanely cute creatures in Phillip Island, an island that is located off the coast of the Victoria region of the country. Each night at sunset, the penguins return to shore after a day of fishing, and watching this "penguin parade" is one of the most magical things you are ever likely to see, in Australia or anywhere else in the world for that matter.

(www.visitphillipisland.com)

26. Take a Trip to Stunning Ayers Rock

Australia has an incredible breadth of landscapes and one of the most unique rock formations in the

Australian desert has to be Ayers Rock, also known by the Aboriginal name of Uluru, close to Alice Springs. This sandstone rock is gargantuan with a height of 348 metres and a total circumference of 9.4 kilometres. The rock also transforms into different colours at different times of the day, and takes on a beautifully warm red at dawn and sunset. There are special viewing areas outside so you can get the best possible photograph of geological wonder.

27. Camp Under the Stars in Wollemi National Park

In Australia, there are plenty of places to reconnect with nature, and more national parks than you can even count. Wollemi National Park is a huge area with deep valleys, canyons, forests, cliffs, and waterfalls. One of the best things about this park, however, is that there's an awesome campground right beside a river. If you really want to zone out from 21st century life, take river walks by the day and then sleep under the stars for a magical experience in nature.

28. View All of Melbourne on the Melbourne Star

Melbourne is a lovely looking city but it's difficult to appreciate just how great it is when you are looking at the city from the ground. But if you want to see Melbourne from the skies, a ride on the Melbourne Star is the perfect thing. This giant Ferris wheel has a height of 120 metres, and once you reach the top, you will be able to see 40 kilometres into the distance, including the harbour area, Phillip Bay, and Arthur's Seat.

(101 Waterfront Way, Docklands VIC; www.melbournestar.com)

29. Look For Birds on the Capertee Valley Bird Trail

As a country with lots of climates and landscapes, Australia plays host to a huge variety of wildlife, and you'll miss out on seeing lots of this wildlife if you fail to look to the skies as there are many types of birds to be found in Australia. If you are a keen birdwatcher, the Capertee Valley Bird Trail is the ultimate place for you. This is recognised as one of the top 50 birdwatching places in the world, and you can see the Regent Honeyeater, the Red-rumped Parrots, and over 200 more bird species besides.

30. Indulge an Inner Hippie at Rabbit Eats Lettuce

If you think of yourself as something of a hippie, the place to find your tribe is at the Rabbit Eats Lettuce festival. The festival is a celebration of freedom, love, and dance music that takes over the NSW coast every Easter across 4 days and nights. If you want to party all night, you have that option, and if you want to chill and make new friends, you can find yoga classes, massage, dance classes, healing sessions, permaculture courses, and lots more coolness out in nature.

(www.rabbitseatlettuce.com.au)

31. Have an African Adventure at Werribee Open Range Zoo

Of course, you wouldn't associate an African adventure with Australia, and yet Werribee Open Range Zoo, which lies around 45 minutes outside of Melbourne, is one of the very best spots in the world for a safari in our opinion. At this zoo, you'll find an incredible array of wild animals living on 225 acres of open savannah. On a safari, you'll get up close to zebra, giraffe, ostrich, rhinoceros, hippo, camel, lion, and more besides.

(K Rd, Werribee South VIC; www.zoo.org.au/werribee)

32. Stroll Though Fremantle Prison, a Former Jail

While visiting a prison on your trip to Australia might seem like a gruesome thing to do, we actually think that Fremantle Prison is one of the most impressive cultural institutions in the country. Constructed in 1855, Fremantle Prison was built as a prison for convicts with convict labour, and it was also the country's only legal place for execution for more than a century. These days, you can walk around the former prison, and see over 15,000 objects related to prison life.

(1 The Terrace, Fremantle WA; http://fremantleprison.com.au)

33. Go Snorkelling at Shoalwater Islands Marine Park

If you really want to experience the beauty of Australia's marine life, a trip to the Shoalwater Islands Marine Park, which lies about an hour south of Perth, is a must visit destination. The water here is perfectly clear, which makes it the ideal destination for snorkelling adventures. Put your head below the water in the reef area, and you will find sea stars, sea urchins, molluscs, and a huge variety of colourful tropical fish. *(153 Arcadia Dr, Rockingham WA)*

34. Indulge With Decadent Ice Cream at Candied Bakery

The summers of Australia can be swelteringly hot, and what better way is there to cool down then with a decadent scoop (or three) of ice cream? The soft serve ice cream at Candied Bakery is the softest and the creamiest in all of Melbourne, and it can be combined with decadent toppings like cookie dough, cookie crumbles, and salted caramel. And if you happen to visit in the winter time, a slice of their pumpkin pie goes down very easily.

(81A Hudsons Rd, Spotswood VIC; http://candiedbakery.com.au)

35. Try Mountain Biking Through John Forrest National Park

If your idea of the perfect trip away is to be immersed in nature as much as possible, Australia is the destination for you because this country seems to have endless national parks, and John Forrest National Park, just outside of Perth, is one of the most treasured. As you might expect from the name, the park is home to lots of beautiful forest land, and something that we really like about the park is that there are quite a few well marked bike trails, so if you really want to raise your adrenaline, you can rent a bike and whizz through the forest.

(https://parks.dpaw.wa.gov.au/park/john-forrest)

36. Dance Til Dawn at the Chinese Laundry

As the most populous city in Australia with almost 5 million inhabitants, Sydney is a place where you can experience killer parties every night of the week, and our favourite place to shimmy until the sun comes up has to be an iconic club called Chinese Laundry. There are different parties to be enjoyed on every week, and plenty of space to dance with three dancefloors and a courtyard for partying outside in the summer months. *(111 Sussex St, Sydney NSW; http://chineselaundryclub.com.au)*

37. Take a Ride on the Kuranda Scenic Railway

While it's true that Australia has many beautiful landscapes and offers plenty of opportunities to be in nature, sometimes you just don't fancy a gruelling hike, and that is when you take a ride on the Kuranda Scenic Railway. This railway runs from Cairns in Queensland to Kuranda, and it takes it many beautiful sights along the way. You will chug along through dense rainforests, gushing waterfalls, and deep ravines for a journey you'll never forget.

(126-144 Bunda St, Cairns City; www.ksr.com.au)

38. Get Historic at the Berndt Museum of Anthropology

Australia as we know it today is a fairly new country, but there is an indigenous culture in Australia that dates back much further in time. If you want to get to grips with aboriginal Australia, we can highly recommend a trip to the Berndt Museum of Anthropology in Perth. The collection contains over 11,500 objects and 32,000 photographs pertaining to indigenous culture. There are also many events and talks at the museum if you want to expand your learning even further.

(35 Stirling Hwy, Crawley WA;
www.culturalprecinct.uwa.edu.au/ venues/galleries-and-
museums/berndt-museum)

39. Be Stunned by the Lesmurdie Falls

If you find yourself in Perth and you want to escape city life for a day, nothing quite beats a trip to the Lesmurdie Falls, the most impressive waterfalls in the region. The hike to get to the waterfalls within Lesmurdie Falls National Park takes just 1-3 hours so it isn't very strenuous, and the views once you arrive at the viewing platform are an incredible reward. There's also parking at the bottom of the falls if you don't feel so adventurous.

(http://trailswa.com.au/trails/lesmurdie-falls)

40. Take in the Smooth Sounds of the Melbourne International Jazz Festival

While Melbourne is certainly not the birthplace of Jazz, not even close, this is not to say that you can't enjoy the smooth sounds of jazz in Australia's cultural city, particularly if you make it to Melbourne in June when the Melbourne International Jazz Festival takes place. Across those two weeks in June, the city buzzes with the spirit of jazz, and there are performances in jazz clubs, concert halls, arts venues, and even on the city streets, with talent being drawn from right around the world.

(http://melbournejazz.com)

41. Get Crafty at the Hawthorn Craft Market

If you find yourself in your last few days in Australia and you have yet to buy anything for yourself or for friends and family at home, a trip to the Hawthron Craft Market in Melbourne might be in order. This market takes place on the first Sunday of each month, and it's a place where you can find craft items you just wouldn't find in high street shops. Along the many stalls, you'll find hand crafted beauty items, unique jewellery and accessories, homeware, prints, and lots more besides.

(City of Boroondora Parkview Room, 340 Camberwell Rd, Camberwell VIC; http://hawthorncraftmarket.org.au)

42. Abseil From Brisbane's Story Bridge

One of the most iconic structures in Brisbane is undoubtedly the Story Bridge, from which you can achieve an incredible view of the river and of the city. But you can do more than simply walk across the bridge. If you fancy yourself as something of a daredevil, you can actually abseil from it. First of all, you get the opportunity to climb the bridge, which is an adventure in itself, and then you can leverage your way down the 30 metre front on a rope. Pretty cool.

(www.sbac.net.au)

43. Indulge a History Buff at the National Museum of Australia

What better place to learn about the ins and outs of Australia than at the National Museum of the country, which is located in the capital city, Canberra? This museum tells the social history of Australia exceptionally well, and inside you'll find a wide range of exhibitions, from displays on bush fires to surf lifesaving. You'll find the world's largest collection of Aboriginal tools and bark paintings. And there are also many interactive displays so that kids will be kept entertained.

(Lawson Cres, Acton; www.nma.gov.au)

44. Enjoy a Camel Safari in Broome

You might associate camels more strongly with countries like Egypt or India, but remember that Australia has all kinds of landscapes and climates, and camels can be found in the Australian desert too. Broome is actually a beach town in the Kimberley region, which is often not on the list of tourists visiting Australia. In our opinion, this is all the more reason to take a trip there, and a camel safari at sunset on the golden sand of the beach only seals the deal.

45. Climb One of the Glass House Mountains

If you fancy yourself as something of an adventurer, and you love to immerse yourself in the great outdoors, Australia is a really fantastic country to visit. There are plenty of hiking opportunities out in the wild, and we are particularly taken by the Glass House Mountains, a series of eleven hills. Probably the most popular of the mountains for climbing is Mount Ngungun. There is a well defined tracks, and while there are steep parts, it's generally not too difficult to complete, and the 360 degree views at the top are spectacular.

46. Spend the Night in the Country's Only Monastic Community

New Norcia is the only Monastic community in all of Australia, where monks live and work together in a spiritual community. If your idea of a great vacation is to get away from the stresses and responsibilities of 21st century life, a stay in the Benedictine Monastery could be just the ticket. The guesthouse in the monastery has 24 rooms, and staying there you'll be invited to join in with monastic activities and enjoy a simpler way of life. *(Great Northern Highway New Norcia Wa; www.newnorcia.wa.edu.au)*

47. Discover the Dugongs of Shark Bay

Shark Bay is western Australia has lots of exceptional natural features, and this has attracted lots of incredible marine life. Something that can be found in Shark Bay in abundance is the dugong. In fact, the bay alone supports 10% of the dugong population. If you've not heard of the dugong before, it's a very unique looking marine mammal. It can be a wonderful idea to take a boat out on to the sea to see these rare and beautiful creatures.

48. Chow Down at the Adelaide Central Market

When it's lunchtime in Adelaide and you want to fill your stomach with extra special, skip the expensive restaurants and head to Adelaide Central Market instead, which is the ultimate food hub for hungry locals. As well as a place to buy fresh produce, there are stalls serving up complete meals, pastries, desserts, and coffees. What's more, the market stays open late on a Friday night, when there is live music to accompany your market grub.

(100 Rundle Mall, Adelaide SA;
www.adelaidecentralplaza.com.au)

49. Be Wowed by Ancient Limestone Formations, The Pinnacles

If you want to see something that's truly one of a kind on your trip to Australia, The Pinnacles, strange limestone formations that can be found in the Nambung National Park need to be high on your Australia bucket list. These strange jagged formations jut out from the earth in a way that no other rocks do on the planet, and scientists still don't quite know why. Why not head out there and take a look for yourself? *(Pinnacles Drive, Cervantes WA)*

50. Prance in the Grass at Splendour in the Grass

If you want to discover the summer festival scene in Australia, a good place to start is the Splendour in the Grass festival, which takes place every July in Byron Bay, and is a music and arts festival that has something for everyone. The stages attract world class talent such as Sigur Ros, Years & Years, Moby, and PJ Harvey, but if live music doesn't do it for you, there's also plenty of street food trucks, yoga, and even circus performances.

51. Discover the Sand Dunes of Fraser Island

Located off the coast of Queensland, Fraser Island is actually the largest sand island in the world. There is plenty to explore, but our highlight always has to be the sand dunes. Not only are the sand dunes absolutely stunning, but one of the sand dunes on the island is dated to being 700,000 years old, which would make it the oldest sand dune sequence in the world. If you want to escape the mainland and get away from it all, this is the place.

(www.fraserisland.net)

52. Visit a Beautiful Waterfall, Mackenzie Falls

Nothing quite beats standing in front of a majestic waterfall as the waters cascade down, and one of the most beautiful waterfalls in Australia has to be Mackenzie Falls in Victoria. The waterfall has an impressive height of around 35 metres, but the really wonderful things is that it has an impressive flow for pretty much the whole year. Trekking to the waterfall inside Grampians National Park takes about an hour and it's a fairly easy hike.

(Northern Grampians Rd, Zumsteins VIC)

53. Have the Best Burger of Your Life at Ziggy's Eatery

Okay, so you haven't travelled all the way to Australia just to try burgers, but let's face it, sometimes all you want to do is chow down on a juicy slab of beef in between toasted bread buns. And when that desire strikes, you need to pay a visit to Ziggy's Eatery in Melbourne. The burgers here are bigger than anywhere else in the city, and that's a good place to start. The double beef with double cheese and double bacon ticks all the boxes, just don't beat yourself up if you can't finish the whole thing.

(195 Carlisle St, Balaclava VIC; http://ziggyseatery.com.au)

54. Take in the Views From the Skyrail Rainforest Cableway

If you fancy exploring the dense rainforest of Queensland in a really unique way, we can highly recommend taking a ride on the Skyrail Rainforest Cableway, a cable journey above the trees that will take you through 7.5 kilometres of absolutely stunning scenery. A return journey takes 2.5 hours, and in that time, you'll see things that you've never seen before as you experience the bird life in the canopy of the jungle and the spectacular views of the rainforest canopy from a great height.

(Captain Cook Hwy & Cairns Western Arterial Road, Smithfield QLD; www.skyrail.com.au)

55. Enjoy a Relaxed Day of Fishing on Lake Wallace

Some people like to have hair raising adventures, and some people are content with sitting on the edge of a lake with a fishing rod. If you are the latter type of person, waste no time in heading to Lake Wallace where you'll find a lake full of trout, specifically rainbow trout, during the high season. You are also permitted to take a sail boat out on to the lake to try and reach those fish in the centre of the lake, and to simply enjoy the peace and quiet of the water.

56. Kick Back With a Movie at The Astor

Yes, it's true that Australia is a country packed full of exciting adventures and attractions, but there are times, even in Australia, when all you want to do is kick back and watch a great movie. When that moment strikes, you head to the iconic Astor cinema in Melbourne. This is an art deco, independent, single screen cinema that plays all the iconic old films on 70mm film. It also has a traditional candy bar where you can stock up on sweet cinema snacks.

(1 Chapel St & Dandenong Rd, Melbourne VIC; www.astortheatre.net.au)

57. Have a Golfing Adventure in Tasmania

If your idea of a perfect getaway is finding the local golf course and hitting a few balls, you'll have no problems finding somewhere to play in Australia because this country is rammed full of courses. While there are more than 100 courses to choose from around Australia, we think that Barnbougle Dunes Golf Links in Tasmania might just be the greatest of them all. This is an 18 hole championship course that is set amongst undulating sand dunes, making this a challenging and unique landscape for playing golf.

(429 Waterhouse Rd, Bridport TAS; http://barnbougle.com.au)

58. Watch an Outdoor Concert at The Domain

Sydney has no shortage of cultural venues, but if you are visiting in the spring or summer months, you probably want to spend as much time outdoors as possible. Fortunately, The Domain is an outdoor venue that blends nature and culture. There are many outdoor cultural events hosted here, from outdoor plays and concerts during the Sydney Festival through to the annual Opera in the Park event. Be sure to keep up to date with their programme.

(2 St Marys Rd, Sydney NSW)

59. Go Sea Kayaking in Freycinet National Park

Lying on the east coast of Tasmania, Freycinet National Park takes up a huge amount of this stretch of coastline, with incredible granite peaks, stunning beaches, and beautiful waters. One of the most popular tourist activities here is to go on a sea kayaking tour. The really nice thing about sea kayaking is that you get to experience the incredibly turquoise waters and really immerse yourself in the landscape, and no prior experience is needed at all.

(Coles Bay Rd, Coles Bay TAS)

60. Tuck Into Fish & Chips at Boathouse Palm Beach

When you are by the coast, and when you are in Australia you will often be by the coast, there is nothing quite like tucking into a freshly made serving of fish and chips, with fluffy chips and crispy battered fish caught from the coast that day. For our money, the best spot in Sydney for Fish & Chips is Boathouse Palm Beach every single time. The fish is beer battered, which makes it beautifully aerated, and if you return for a second visit, the bucket of prawns is delicious as well. *(Governor Phillip Park, Barrenjoey Rd, Palm Beach NSW; www.theboathousepb.com.au)*

61. Enjoy Some Zen at Himeji Gardens

While it should be said that Adelaide is not the most bustling city on the planet, if you still feel as though you need some peace, quiet, and nature, we can recommend a trip to the Himeji Gardens in the city. Himeji is the sister city of Adelaide in Japan, and these gardens were a gift from the twin city. Inside, you'll find an ornamental lake with water lilies, a rock garden, and even a teahouse where you can relax with some green tea.

(South Terrace, Adelaide SA)

62. Raise Your Adrenaline by Rafting on the North Johnstone River

Yes, Australia has incredible landscapes, but you can do better than just taking photos of the mountains and rivers, and actually immerse yourself in landscapes of the country. The North Johnstone River is probably the most popular place in Australia for a white water rafting adventure. In fact, this river has grades four and five rapids, and this means that the water really gushes, and you are bound to have a hair raising experience you will never forget.

63. Find Something Special at Melbourne's Bend and Snap Market

Melbourne is a creative city through and through, and you can really feel the creative pulse of Melbourne at the Bend and Snap Market. This market only takes place a few times a year, and it's the time of the year when all local designers, craft makers, and creatives get to showcase their wares. At each market you can find unique fashions, works from textile artists, hand crafted jewellery, and lots more besides. This might just be the place for you to do all your souvenir shopping.

(https://bendandsnapmarket.wordpress.com)

64. Discover Australia's Seafaring Heritage at Queensland Maritime Museum

Located on the southern bank of the Brisbane river, the Queensland Maritime Museum is a place where you can really get to grips with the maritime heritage of the country. Inside the museum, you can find historic ship models from early cargo ships through to modern container ships. You'll also find many artefacts related to maritime culture, as well as information about the 1500 shipwrecks that have occurred along the Queensland coast, including the Barrier Reef.

(412 Stanley St, South Brisbane QLD;

https://maritimemuseum.com.au)

65. See in the New Year at Field Day

Australians love to party, and this mean that it can be a great idea to be in the country around New Year. And if you really want to experience a New Year's Day that you will never forget, you should know about the Field Day festival, which is hosted on New Year's Day each year in a Sydney Park. Each year, there is a cool mix of indie, pop, and dance talent, so everyone can enjoy themselves. Acts that have previously taken to the stage include Calvin Harris, Chance the Rapper, and Bastille.

66. Hit the Slopes of Mount Buller

When you think of countries around the world that are great for skiing, you might first think of Canada, France, or Japan, but probably not Australia. But actually, Australia is such a vast country that you can find pretty much every type of climate and every type of landscape, and if you head to Mount Buller, you will find slopes that are perfect for skiing and snowboarding. In fact, the ski resort there is well established, and you might even want to try some new adventures like bobsledding or night skiing.
(www.mtbuller.com.au)

67. Wave a Rainbow Flag for Sydney Gay & Lesbian Mardi Gras

Although Australia is firmly part of the western world, it hasn't quite caught up with the world when it comes to LGBT rights. Same sex sexual activity was only made legal in 1994, and same sex marriage is still not legal in the country. With that said, there is a very visible LGBT community and a thriving gay scene, and never is this more apparent than at the annual Sydney Gay & Lesbian Mardi Gras, hosted each year in March. Highlights of the festival include Drag Races on Bondi Beach, a Mardia Gras Film Festival, and parades through the street.

(www.mardigras.org.au)

68. Find Something Special at Gilles Street Market, Adelaide

Although it's held in the playground of a local school, Gilles Street Market has actually built a reputation as one of the best markets in all of Australia. This market is held on the third Sunday of every month, and the beauty of the market is that you'll find something different there each and every month. Stallholders sell things like vintage fashions and hand crafted jewellery, there are numerous food stalls, and there are often DJs so you can even have a daytime dance.

(91 Giles St, Adelaide SA; http://gillesstreetmarket.com.au)

69. Be Wowed by St Paul's Cathedral in Melbourne

When you think of countries around the world with spectacular church architecture, Australia probably isn't the first country that pops into your head. As a relatively young country, it's true that you won't find 1000 year old churches, but there are some very fine examples of church architecture nonetheless. The location of the St Paul's in Melbourne marks the spot of the first Christian service in the city 1835, but the church wasn't built until 1891. If you have the chance to see an organ recital in this church, grab it with both hands.

(Flinders Ln & Swanston St, Melbourne VIC; https://cathedral.org.au)

70. Taste Australian Wines in Swan Valley

The Yarra Valley might be the best known of the wine regions in Australia, but the Swan Valley is the oldest, and this is where the story of Australian wines first started. There are around 40 wineries in the region and many of them are small family run affairs where you can chat with multiple generations who work on the land. Why not pass a few days staying in the vineyards with al fresco lunches and wine tastings to remember?

71. Sail Around the Whitsunday Islands

Australia is, of course, an island in itself, but there are also many picturesque smaller islands dotted around the coast of the country. The Whitsunday Islands is a collection of 74 islands that are sheltered by the Great Barrier Reef, and in our opinion, the waters of these islands provide some of the very best sailing on the planet. Whether you stay on one of the islands and take a sailing day trip or you create a whole vacation on the waters, just make sure you don't leave this part of Australia unexplored.

(www.tourismwhitsundays.com.au)

72. Learn Something at the Tandanya National Aboriginal Culture Institute

If you find yourself in Adelaide, and you would like to experience some culture, the Tandanya National Aboriginal Culture Institute is definitely the place to be. Tandanya was opened in 1989, and it serves as a place to explore both traditional and contemporary indigenous expression. There is an art gallery inside, as well as regular dance and music performances. The shop is also a great place to purchase souvenirs made by local indigenous people.

(253 Grenfell St, Adelaide SA; www.tandanya.com.au)

73. Take in a Rugby Match at Suncorp Stadium

Australia is a sporty nation, and one particular sport that is very popular here is rugby. If you think of yourself as a sporty kind of person, it can be a great idea to take a day out and actually see a rugby match being played. There are plenty of awesome rugby stadiums all over the country, but we particularly like the Suncorp Stadium, which is located in the suburbs of Brisbane. This stadium can fit up to 52,000 people, and when it is full the atmosphere is electric.

(40 Castlemaine St, Milton QLD;
www.suncorpstadium.com.au)

74. Get Cultural at the Annual Sydney Festival

If you are a culture buff, you are going to fall in love with the museums and galleries of Sydney, but the city's cultural scene really comes to life during January when the whole city is taken over by the annual Sydney Festival. There is something to suit everyone, so whether you'd like to see classical music performances, contemporary dances, art shows, comedy, circus, or anything else that falls under the umbrella of "culture", you will be in luck.

(www.sydneyfestival.org.au)

75. Get Close to Crocodiles at Daintree River

The Daintree River is a river that winds through the rainforest, and as you might imagine, this means that there is an abundance of incredible wildlife living both in and around the river. One of the most notorious creatures that exists here is the crocodile, and you can actually take specific boat trips on the river that will allow you to get close (but not too close) to these amazing animals. You might also see tree snakes, birdlife, and lots of incredible rainforest.

76. Indulge an Inner Shopaholic on Chapel Street

If your idea of great time in a new country is shopping until you have maxed out your credit card, we'd like to introduce you to Chapel Street in Melbourne. This street is the shopping hub of Melbourne, and it's the kind of place where you can find anything and everything. One of our favourite shops one the street is Olga de Polga, a vintage shop full of loud prints and modern cuts that will make you stand out from the crowd. And Chapel St Bazaar is a junk shop in the most traditional sense – you might just walk away with some treasure.

77. Start Your Day With Coffee From Little Bean Blue

Are you the kind of person who can't function without your first coffee of the day? If so, Australia will feel like heaven for you because this is a nation of hardcore coffee lovers. But when you're in a new place, it's hard to separate the good coffee from the bad. Luckily you have us to advise you, and when in Melbourne, believe us when we say that Little Bean Blue is the place to be. The staff are very knowledgeable, so if you need help deciding on your roast don't hesitate to ask for some guidance.

(15 Little Collins St, Melbourne VIC)

78. Go Diving in the Great Barrier Reef

The Great Barrier Reef is the world's largest coral reef system anywhere on the planet, and this makes Australia a must visit destination for diving enthusiasts. Whether you love to dive, or this will be your first time, there is no chance of the Great Barrier Reef being a disappointment. On every dive you will see something different. You have the chance of seeing cuttlefish, Minke whales, green sea turtles, barracudas, and of course lots of beautiful and colourful coral.

79. Take in the Spectacular View on the Wheel of Brisbane

If you fancy seeing the city of Brisbane from a very unique vantage point, we can heartily recommend taking a ride on the Wheel of Brisbane, the city's official Ferris wheel. As you embark on this journey, you will be taken 60 metres into the air so that you can have a 360 degree view of everything around you. You can guarantee that your holiday snaps taken from the Wheel of Brisbane will be something extra special.

(Russel Street, South Brisbane QLD; www.thewheelofbrisbane.com.au)

80. Take in a Gig at Melbourne's Cherry Bar

If you find yourself in Melbourne in the evening time and at a loss of what to do, we can recommend a trip to the iconic Cherry Bar, which is one of the most popular spots for live music in the city. This bar opened in 2000, and you can expect different kinds of music on each night of the week, so whether you're into rock or soul, you should find something to suit you. When Noel Gallagher visited the place, he was so enamoured with Cherry Bar that he made an offer to buy it.

(Acdc Ln, Melbourne VIC; http://cherrybar.com.au)

81. Get to Grips With Contemporary Art at Carriageworks

If you find yourself in Sydney with the desire to explore the cultural side of the city, you have more than a few options, but one of our favourite cultural places in the city has to be Carriageworks. If you really want to get to grip with contemporary art in the city, this gallery has its finger on the pulse, and one of its temporary exhibits shouldn't be missed. There are also events like art performances, film screenings, and readings in the venue.

(245 Wilson St, Eveleigh NSW; http://carriageworks.com.au)

82. Tour the Smiling Samoyed Brewery

Something that you'll discover sooner rather than later in Australia is that the local people certainly are fond of beer. While you'll have absolutely no trouble finding delicious lagers and ales around the country it can be especially fun to visit one of the country's many microbreweries, and the Smiling Samoyed Brewery is always at the top of our list. This brewery has its own bar overlooking the Myponga Reservoir, and in the winter you are invited to warm up next to their wood fire.

(48 Main S Rd, Myponga SA; www.smilingsamoyed.com.au)

83. Keep Kids Happy at the Interactive Museum, Questacon

Travelling with kids is no easy thing. We all know that keeping kids entertained on trips away is easier said than done, but you won't have to worry too much in Australia, particularly if you take them on a trip to Questacon in Canberra, which is the National Science and Technology Centre. Inside the doors of this interactive museum, there are more than 200 experiences to be had, from freezing your own shadow through to experiencing a simulated earthquake.

(King Edward Terrace, Parkes ACT; www.questacon.edu.au)

84. Celebrate Chinese New Year in Sydney

The ultimate place to celebrate Chinese New Year is, of course, in China, but we think that Sydney comes in at a close second. In fact, each year there are around 70 celebratory events for the New Year in Sydney, and 1 million people join in with the festivities. One of the highlights of the New Year celebrations has to be the lighting of 12 incredible Zodiac lanterns around the city, where Chinese communities based in Australia and China put on incredible dance, theatre, and music shows.

85. Visit the Stunning Limestone Stacks, The Twelve Apostles

Australia is full of unique geological formations, and The Twelve Apostles is certainly something that you can only see in Australia. Located off the coast of

Victoria, these are limestone formations that dramatically jut out from the sea, and are caused by the dramatic sea erosion of the area. Originally there were limestone caves, these gave way to arches, and were eventually eroded down to stacks, some of which are 50 metres in height.

86. Chow Down at the Taste of Tasmania

What exactly constitutes Tasmanian food? It's fair to say that food from the Tasmania region of Australia isn't world famous, but that's not to say it isn't good, and you can discover all the goodness of this local grub at the annual Taste of Tasmania festival, which is hosted at the end of December and beginning of January. Whether you want to relax with a day sipping on chilled wines, or you'd prefer to nibble on all the local cheese produced in the area, this foodie festival will offer something for you.

(www.thetasteoftasmania.com.au)

87. Meet New People and Volunteer at a Hostel

There is no denying that Australia is one of the more expensive countries in the world, and that might make it seem prohibitive for budget travellers, but actually, with a little imagination and smart thinking, Australia can be experienced with getting in trouble with your bank manager. We are in love with the workaway.com website. On this website, you can find many hostel owners around Australia (and worldwide) who need people to help out in their hostels for around 4-5 hours a day in exchange for room and board. Plus you'll get to meet other travellers, and have a cool work experience to put on your CV.

(www.workaway.com)

88. Get Close to Marine Life at Sea Life Sydney Aquarium

As a country totally surrounded by water, Australia does of course have an astounding variety of marine life in its waters. If you would like to get up close to some of this sea life while in Sydney, we can recommend a trip to the Sea Life Sydney Aquarium. The aquarium plays host to over 700 fish and sea life species, and more than 13,000 individual fish and sea creatures. We particularly love the Shark Valley oceanarium with its underwater tunnels you can walk through.

(1-5 Wheat Rd, Sydney NSW; www.sydneyaquarium.com.au)

89. Stay on a Working Pearl Farm

When you go on holiday, you most likely stay in hotels, guesthouses, or hostels, but do a bit of digging and you can make your accommodation experience a hundred times more exciting, like how about staying on a working pearl farm? Yup, that is a genuine option at Cygnet Bay Pearl Farm in Kimberley. This farm has its own stunning cottages on-site, and while you are there you can learn about the pearling industry and enjoy the beautiful coastline.

(Cape Leveque Road, Dampier Peninsula WA; www.cygnetbaypearls.com.au)

90. Roll Around Laughing at the Melbourne International Comedy Festival

There is nothing quite as fun as laughing until you can't laugh any more, and if you want to experience a few belly laughs of your own, it can be a great idea to time your trip to Australia to coincide with the Melbourne International Comedy Festival. At this festival, you are bound to find a stand-up show or sketch comedy to suit you because it's the third largest comedy festival on the planet. It takes place every March, and there's typically more than 450 shows.

(www.comedyfestival.com.au)

91. Enjoy a Decadent Meal at Sydney Restaurant, Quay

While it is true that Australia can sometimes be on the expensive side, sometimes you simply have to throw caution to the wind and really indulge. And if it's indulgence that you are after, we can't think of many restaurants around the country more indulgent than Quay in Sydney. From the restaurant, you have the most perfect vista of Sydney Harbour, but even so it's

the food that really makes Quay stand out. The tasting
menu will give you a bite of all the goodies, including
Murray cod and succulent Australian lamb.
(Overseas Passenger Terminal, Hickson Rd, The Rocks NSW;
www.quay.com.au)

92. Party in the Australian Bush for Strawberry Fields

If you have some inner hippie tendencies, we think that
you might be enamoured by the Strawberry Fields
festival, which is hosted for 3 days each November in
the Australian Bush outside of Melbourne. This festival
will give you the opportunity to dance til you drop to
the coolest electronica music, but if you'd rather not
party, you can also take it easy with yoga and
meditation workshops, art installations, and stalls where
you can buy hand crafted items.
(www.strawberry-fields.com.au)

93. See Wildlife in the Open at Healesville Sanctuary

There is plenty of wildlife to be found all over Australia, but instead of taking your chances in one of the gargantuan national parks, why not guarantee that you'll be able to see some spectacular wildlife on your trip by paying a visit to the Healesville Sanctuary, which is located in rural Victoria? This zoo specialises in animals that are native to Australia, and once in the sanctuary you can get up close to wombats, dingoes, kangaroos, and many bird species.

(Badger Creek Rd, Healesville VIC; www.zoo.org.au/healesville)

94. Enjoy a Quiet Moment at the Church of St Stephen, Brisbane

While Australia might not be a country that is very famous for its church architecture, this is certainly not to say that there are not some stunning churches dotted around the country, and the Church of St Stephen in Brisbane happens to be one of our favourites. This Catholic church took a long time to build and was constructed between the years of 1864 and 1922. Something really special about this church is that it has three choirs, and it's a wonderful place to take in a traditional concert.

(249 Elizabeth St, Brisbane City QLD; http://cathedralofststephen.org.au)

95. Indulge a Cheese Fanatic at the Milawa Cheese Company

One of the best things about visiting a new country for the first time is sampling lots of the local food, and while Australia might not be world famous for its cheese production, we don't believe that any cheese lovers will be disappointed on a trip here. If you are a cheese fanatic to your core, we highly recommend stopping in at the Milawa Cheese Company in Milawa, Victoria. You can actually take a trip to the farm and see some cheese making in action, and of course, take some of the good stuff home with you.

(www.milawacheese.com.au)

96. Dance to the Best Electronic Music at Subsonic

If you love nothing more than to dance to heavy beats and the sickest electronica out there, you will fall head over heels for Subsonic festival, which takes place 3 hours north of Sydney in early December when Australia is in the height of summer. If you don't fancy roughing it in a grubby campsite, this festival has some of the best glamping that we've ever seen, with an awesome site next to the river and hot showers to boot. *(www.subsonic.org)*

97. Discover Aboriginal Art at the National Gallery of Australia

While Australia as we know it is a fairly new country, there is an Aboriginal culture that dates back far longer, and if you really want to get to grips with Australia, you have to appreciate this indigenous culture. One place to get under the skin of this part of Australia is at the National Gallery of Australia in Canberra, where you can find more than 166,000 works of art, including a great deal of indigenous art. The sculpture garden is also a wonderful place for a stroll.

(Parkes Pl, Parkes ACT; http://nga.gov.au)

98. Get Back to Nature at Sydney's Royal Botanic Gardens

When you find yourself in Sydney and you want to escape the hustle and bustle of the big city, you can't do much better than taking a morning out and walking around the stunning Royal Botanic Gardens. The gardens opened way back in 1816, making them the oldest scientific institution in the country. Covering over 70 acres, inside you will find a rare and threatened plant garden, a rainforest walk, a rose garden, a herb garden, relaxing ponds, and much more besides.

(Mrs Macquaries Rd, Sydney NSW; www.rbgsyd.nsw.gov.au)

99. Sip on Cocktails at Bulletin Place

It's in the evening time that Sydney really comes to life, and if you fancy sipping on a cocktail or two, Sydney has loads of places that serve up great drinks. We think, however, that Bulletin Place might just be the best of them all. This shoebox sized bar has distressed walls and bare bulbs, but the drinks are altogether more decadent. We can recommend the Rhuby Tuesday, which contains rhubarb, triple sec, lemon, and Cognac – delicious!

(10-14 Bulletin Pl, Sydney NSW; https://bulletinplace.com)

100. Delve into the Central Deborah Goldmine

Bendigo is a very important place for industry in Australia, because between 1850 and 1900, more gold was excavated there than from any other place in the world. You can discover this illustrious history for yourself by taking a trip into the Central Deborah Goldmine. The most extreme experience takes you 228 metres below the ground in an authentic mining tunnel. You'll be kitted out in a miner's uniform, and you'll be taught all the tricks of the trade.

(76 Violet St, Bendigo VIC; www.central-deborah.com)

101. Take in 360 Degree Views From Split Point Lighthouse

The Great Ocean Road in Victoria is one of the most celebrated coastal drives in the world, and as you drive along this stretch of coastline, you are sure to find yourself face to face with the dominating Split Point Lighthouse. This lighthouse was built in 1891, but has only opened for tours since 2013. Since then, people have enjoyed climbing to the top and enjoying the stunning 360 degree panoramic view.

(Federal St, Aireys Inlet VIC;
http://splitpointlighthouse.com.au)

Before You Go...

Thanks for reading **101 Coolest Things to Do in Australia.** We hope that it makes your trip a memorable one!

Keep your eyes peeled on www.101coolestthings.com, and have a wonderful time Down Under.

Team 101 Coolest Things

Printed in Great Britain
by Amazon